HUMAN ECOLOGY:
NOTES ON THE SACRED ELEMENT WORK

INVOCATION:

*Toward the One,
The Perfection of Love, Harmony and Beauty,
The Only Being
United with All the Illuminated Souls
Who form the embodiment of the Master
The Spirit of Guidance.*

ISBN 0-9781705-6-3
copyright © Carol Sill, 1985, 2006, all rights reserved

Part of this work was published in the periodical, Caravanserai, in the late 1980's.
All quotations from The Sufi Message of Inayat Khan.

Alpha Glyph Publications
www.alphaglyph.com

Human Ecology:
Notes on the Sacred Element Work

Contents

Introductory Notes	3
Symbology and Nature Meditations	4
Steps in Creating the Sacred Element Rituals	5
A Cohesive Spiritual Alchemy	6
Symbology as Translator	8
An Ancient School of Agriculture	9
In the Present Sacred Element Ritual	10
The Place of Ceremony	12
Let Us Gather Again	13
All Words Concerning Symbology	14
A Connected Revival	15
Human Ecology	16
Ecological Balance	19
Training, Ceremony, Art and Education	24
From the Sufi Message of Inayat Khan	27
Elementary School	46
Symbolical Activities	62
Decoding the Symbols	66
Observations	68

Foreword

This slim volume was first written in 1985 after my introduction to the symbolical activity of the sufis. I had heard of this symbolical work in sufi circles but only associated it with "gardening" and felt little interest in it at that time. Then a mention of the connection with Greek mysteries truly piqued my interest, and I soon learned to explore this symbolic work with sacred element rituals at Lake O'Hara Camp, through the guidance of Hidayat Inayat Khan, and with the participation of all who were present at the gatherings. High in the Canadian Rockies at the exquisite and secluded Lake O'Hara Lodge, the ceremony was developed and expressed through movement and sound.

In my efforts to understand the basis of what we were doing, I turned to the collected lectures of Inayat Khan for clarification and clues to the metaphysics of this extraordinary activity. This volume is comprised of my notes and writings during that study. It is an exploration, not a definitive statement.

The ceremony was, for me, a wonderful and intense esoteric workshop - highly creative and totally involving of body, mind, heart and soul. Costumes and robes were created, including elaborate headdresses for the "mothers" of each element, all brought for the ceremonial ritual. Each person who participated was part of an element group - either earth, water, fire, air or ether. Wearing the colour of that element, each group produced an interpretive dance expressing the qualities of that element. Working with these groups in rehearsal gave me insight and inspiration in understanding the various ways of each of the elements. At a certain point in the ritual, the elements combined in a mutual celebratory dance, going from chaos to a peaceful, harmonious and beautiful conclusion.

The conductor of the ceremony wore a simple white robe, while all around the colours swirled - yellow, green, red, blue and grey/violet. The element groups were situated at the points of a five-pointed star, with the conductor at the centre. Observing participants formed a circle around the star, while musicians were off to one side.

At a certain time in the ceremony, the dancing elements in combination formed a unifying spiral of celebration. From free play to unity, the elements in the ritual revealed themselves through the participants who embodied them in dance. It is an ancient method of divine communication.

Since those early days at Lake O'Hara, the ceremony has continued. Others have also taken on the role of "mother" of the elements. It is now a kind of sacred ballet, a beautiful expression, and no doubt more controlled and refined than the exhuberant free-wheeling participatory events we held at O'Hara years ago.

What strikes me now, over twenty years later - aside from my enthusiasm - is just how the vocabulary of element work is central to the understanding of mysticism. After participating in the ceremonial rituals, I have continued this work in an inner way, using those principles that were demonstrated symbolically. I recently rediscovered the work of Dr.O.C.Gruner on the elements and healing, and once again was struck by the realization that he had received this connection directly from his teacher, Pir-O-Murshid Inayat Khan. The basis of all these teachings is open and clearly available in the lectures and papers.

For us now in the 21st century, there is a persistence of knowledge and meaning to be rediscovered. In yoga systems, and many others worldwide, the elements have their place in metaphysics. As colours, directions, breaths, senses, planets, they all intermingle within us and around us to define the soul's experience of life itself.

In one of the papers, Inayat Khan in effect plays the scales, musically introducing the levels of vibration in relation to the individual experience via the senses:

"What touches one's soul least is the experience by sense of touch, the experience by the sense of taste touches deeper, but the experience through the sense of smell has a deeper effect. The experience one receives through the sight reaches deeper still; but the experience that goes into the innermost being of man is that which he receives through the sense of hearing."

And now, the other direction:

"The soul rises to enjoy every experience in life. To see it rises more than it does in hearing, it rises still more in smelling, it must rise higher still in tasting, and it rises to the surface in the sense of touch. It is therefore that the sense of touch makes a greater appeal to the sensitiveness of some than any other experience of life."

I see in this description of differing gradations of sense experience a coded message of the song of the soul, sung in element vibrations as they manifest in our human ecology.

Sufia Carol Sill
Vancouver, 2006

HUMAN ECOLOGY:
NOTES ON THE SACRED ELEMENT WORK

The following notes on Symbology and the Sacred Element ceremony were written (mostly in 1985) for my own exploration, to develop and evolve my understanding of this work. Some aspects of the writing are still in process, but I felt the exploration should be shared with others.

Sufia
Calgary, Alberta
Feb. 5, 1988

Introductory Notes
On the Symbolical Activity
of the Sacred Element Work

The Symbolical Activity was created as a vehicle of the Sufi Message and for the use and encouragement of the students within that endeavour. In the early days, it was left unfinished. I believe, however, that the lines which Pir-O-Murshid Inayat Khan drew for its present and future evolution are available to sincere seekers. Discovery of the hidden Message within this activity is the revelation of the meaning in the symbology: nature covering and uncovering her beauty. It is up to the inspiration of those working in this line to interpret, to develop and to fulfill this hidden Message.

In his biography, Pir-O-Murshid Inayat Khan refers to the groups he formed here and there as "farms" or if they were new and unformed, "fields". He left "the farm" in the care of so-and-so, for example. This terminology indicates his relationship to the symbolical "farm" concept - not as agriculture per se, but as the cultivation of humanity through the growth of the Message of love, harmony and beauty.

Also in his biography, Pir-O-Murshid Inayat Khan stated that the Sufi Message he was destined to give was being carried out in the Movement by diligent but not quite ready workers, yet he maintained admiration and gratitude for all who assisted this cause. His understanding naturally went to symbolism, which as he often said was the way the wise of all ages have given knowledge to humanity. The Symbolical Activity, most inexplicable, is itself a complex symbol which he left for our evolution and inspiration.

In the early Symbolical Activity, as it was being formulated and tried out, he was undoubtedly present, as he was in the Universal Worship, the Confraternity, the Healing Service, the Esoteric School. Each of these activities holds patterns of esoteric value which enable profound communication. The Symbolical work, being another mysterious branch of Sufism, holds a similar living pattern which was begun in Pir-O-Murshid Inayat Khan's presence and continues in the present day.

Without this Symbolical work, the sufi effort is made up of four parts, and makes the sign of the cross, but with it, it becomes the five-pointed star.

The Sacred Element Work heals the inner structure of our lives, and helps to develop and increase a potential 'inner temple' by which can be projected holographic 'types' of the 'perfect forms'.

Symbology and Nature Meditations

In the *Nature Meditations*, Inayat Khan has given us a means of sensing nature as a great anthropomorphic entity, with all its variations as attributes of feeling, love, generosity, etc. The Sacred Element work gives us a tool for discovering that nature which exists in humanity.

These two activities are two aspects of the same intention. For example, in *Nature Meditations*, the seed is evoked: *Thou art the life and thou art life's sustenance,* and the inner being of the seed reveals itself to the keen observer.

All the *Nature Meditations* open this capacity, most particularly those to do with people, which call forth the Person of the Divine Presence. The Symbolical Activity of the Sacred Element Work begins with the human being, and evokes inner meaning to reveal itself to the keen observer.

Symbology was left unfinished, and perhaps it can never be entirely complete. Its work unfolds through time, building the bridge generation by generation.

Sacred Element ceremonies: the worship of God in Human Nature.
Nature Meditations: the assistance of humanity through God as nature.
The worship of God through nature leads to the worship of God through human nature. This leads to the unfoldment of human nature.
The Sacred Ceremony of the Elements is the Message in a symbolic form. When enacted it becomes a body for the evolution of humanity.
Nature Meditations involve the worship of the person behind nature.
These Sacred Rituals involve the worship of all nature in the person.

The Steps in Creating the Sacred Element Work

The steps in creating the Sacred Element work involves a series of inner initiations of earth, water, fire, air and ether. It is necessary for anyone involved to recognize the challenge and to master the element which attempts to overwhelm and overcome the initiate.

This challenge comes to the initiate in his/her everyday life. The form of the challenge will be fashioned from the materials at hand. The labor is to overcome the challenge.

The elements do not challenge in sequence. Usually, the initiate has already overcome part of the challenge of the elements in previous Sufi training. However, it is only in the naked grip of one dominating element after the other that the initiate can wrest the gold from within.

The challenge comes through people and personal circumstances more often than through "nature". For example, fire is not flame; air is not hurricane, etc. The test situation can always be overcome by the correct balance which yields love, harmony and beauty. It is only when the test becomes "the only reality" that the initiate is lost. Even then, the eventual overcoming of the element which threatens supremacy gives to the initiate the power of that element at his/her command, and the loving recognition (mutual) between the element and him/herself forever.

There are differing patterns of confrontation, recognition and overcoming according to the movement, color and pattern of each element's nature.

A Cohesive Spiritual Alchemy

A cohesive spiritual alchemy of the present times is expressed in the Sacred Element work and the adoration of the five elements. It is a clear approach, free from all former historical trappings which have gathered about the alchemical system of understanding the universe over the centuries.

Presently, the yearning for spiritual understanding has shifted in North America to become a desire to go to the root of things. There is a return to traditionalism and a mistrust of charismatic guru figures. The Sacred Element work reveals itself to be a mature western version of one such root teaching. Being western it attracts those who are of this culture, and yearn for that which is deeper, and so seek in the aboriginal beliefs (for example) for the roots of their culture and being.

Through Sacred Element work, the spiritual life of humanity can be renewed. The essence of the Sufi Message is transmitted symbolically through this ceremony. The power of the Sacred Element ceremony is in this essence of the Sufi Message. Without the Message, it could be meaningless, a manipulation of form without life.

Life which is infused in the elements renews human endeavour. Life giving its homage to these elements will renew all humanity. The Sacred Element work can form part of the basis of renewed religious activity of humankind.

In previous ages the hidden power of this knowledge came to accelerate and renew humanity at a time of change, trouble or desperation. This is such a time.

Element symbology in earlier times brought the initial impetus for medical knowledge and for the categorization of phenomena, the beginning of what we now call 'modern science'.

Scientific impulse may seem to have outrun this basis and has created a world which denies the impulse of these archetypical elements. Most scientists in all fields, including psychology, consider the symbolical approach quaint and without present value. [See Dr. Gruner's translation of Avicenna's *Canon of Medicine*.] However, deeper understanding of the elements is completely consistent with modern physics.

When these concepts first introduced themselves into the ancient world, they radically transformed thought and action, and ushered in what can be referred to as a 'new age'.

Aboriginal peoples of the earth have always kept a version of the original impulse of this force, each according to their specific culture. They have not done as we in the west and separated this force from life and ceremony as a means of creating the scientific world of humanist thought. They still understand the elements in the old way, filled with life. This is considered pagan. In the west, a return to a primal pagan state frightens most people. A transition into such a state can paradoxically enhance civilization and encourage renewal if the elements are reintroduced as major players in the events of life. The change is seen not as a return to a primitive primal state, but rather as a retrieval of vitality to be applied to a deeper understanding of present life.

Stripped to basics, the pre-theological life forces can give to our society the impulses necessary to truly bring together the divergent forces now vying for supremacy.

The Sacred Element work is an offering to God, and in no way denies God nor traditional religion. It does not oppose the Christian beliefs and values but is complementary as art and science are complementary in their evolution and direction. Like all aspects of the Sufi Message, the Sacred Element work is a harmonizing force. For without light, without the direct impulse of the Spirit of Guidance as Christ, as Buddha, Krishna, Moses, Mohammed, the Element symbology would not leaven humanity, but sink it, as has happened in the past. The religions may have corrected this, yet they also created their own imbalance over time.

However, without the understanding of these varied forces in action, the religious life in the world can become stagnant and unhelpful. Element symbology infuses the work of Aquinas and all medieval humanists. It prepared the Renaissance.

It is in symbols that the forces of life are allowed free play on the material plane. Down the ages and through time these symbols have their effect unknown to most of humanity. Element symbology is behind them. It can be seen as the agriculture of humanity. The fostering of human growth. The development of the fruit and the seed. The encouragement of life.

The retrieval of this great hidden work is now part of many people's consciousness. In this ferment of thought, the form of the new will come to light. Certain individuals express these symbolic concepts, which are more than ideas. One close analogy to the Element concept-symbol is the Sanskrit word, or letter, or the yogic pre-Sanskrit esoteric language.

These concepts have been suspended out of frame for centuries. Partially leaking through to assist when necessary, they have been withheld from humanity until adequate preparation combined with need caused the circumstances to release the hidden treasure.

Full understanding of Element symbology requires a society which is of that awareness - one which needs the tremendous calm, the realization could be seen as out-of-mind, the total reconnection with all life. Yes, it is a return to "mood-mud" (Joyce) but this symbolic world is in fact highly elaborated and clearly articulated - in every way a higher and more sophisticated communication form.

It develops and includes telepathy, psychic phenomena, worship, meditation, inner peace, religious devotions and purifications. It develops and includes science, physics, medicine, psychology, sociology, anthropology, technology and all disciplines. It develops and includes art, music, drama, ritual, film, video. It develops and includes all forms of human expression, interaction and communication.

The Symbolical Activity's concepts will lead humanity back to the source, back to simplicity in the midst of technological complexity, but without denying the complex reality of present conditions in society.

Symbology as Translator

Translation is the key to all symbolism, to all work referring to the elements. Translation or transposition are inadequate terms to describe the process of Sacred Element symbology as it is introduced into any field. Life living creates this ritual. Recognition of the ritual adds love.

Involvement in the effort to understand symbolical expressions gives a deepening to all life. This broad use of the idea of the Sacred Elements unfolds mysteries for the seeker.

An Ancient School of Agriculture

To call the Symbolical Activity an ancient school of agriculture can be likened to alchemy being an ancient method of creating gold from base metals. This agriculture - is it to be taken literally? Within the Sufi Message of Inayat Khan, all is included in this activity: the understanding of symbolic use of form, of sound, of color, of gesture, of image, of human intention.

That original tradition, based as it was in agriculture, took humanity out of the wandering, hunting phase and into settlement. The secrets of civilization, and of feeding the people, and of creating stable settlements in which the human beings have control over the forces of nature, were held as mysteries.

The cycle of seasons and seasonal rituals were kept pure by the ancients, held as "mysteries" by the Greeks and others. Egyptian initiates were also working in the same field, as were the Aztecs and many others around the world at that time. Each evolved and devolved culturally around this central pre-religious initiatory program. However, it was among the Greeks that it was preserved as the highest of all art forms in the mystery temples. This work can be called "pre-religious" in that it wasn't based on the teachings of a known world prophet. It was "pagan", before the idea of One God had been commonly accepted. It was consistent with the revelations of the Vedic philosophers, and with the early Chinese sages as well.

Despite the masculine focus in Greek culture, in spiritual matters oracles were all women trained by priests. In the mysteries, men and women intermingled freely as priests and priestesses. Of course, as with all cycles, the height of these mysteries coincided with the beginning devolution and decay which many now associate with the Greek Mysteries. In its origin and intention, however, a great purity existed for many centuries. Entrance to the temple's inner rooms was allowed only to initiates, for the general public could not understand. Many initiates themselves did not yet understand the significance of the ritual. The ritual, beyond the spectacle of the oracle, beyond the initiation, was simple and secret: still it is shrouded in mystery, yet it remains alive today.

The Symbolical Activity is nothing less than the worship of God in human nature.

In the Present Sacred Element Ceremony

Each level contains a seed-pattern of evolution for humanity, which, repeated often enough, will eventually take hold.

The first level is simple: an adoration of the elements couched in beauty and reverence.

The next level requires many further inner initiations, which occur in conjunction with the seasons, the moon, the sincerity of the initiate and involve an inner conquest of each of the five elements, so that at the end of the cycle of five, the initiate is able to stand above them all, surveying their work in all creation.

Then the simple ceremony of adoration of the elements takes on a new, deeper meaning, as each element lives before the initiate. Once this stage is completed, the inner initiations involve the manipulation of the elements in artful manner for the glory and renewal of all creation. "Tamed" by the initiate, they will work for him/her to renew the world, an offering to the Divine Presence.

All this process occurs within the initiate, who is learning to recognize, work with, and control these element forces within him/herself. Naturally, this work leads to a fierce love of humanity, because Symbolical Activity is best begun after the full Sufi initiation has occurred. This means that the notion of separated individuality, person to person, is seen simply as a convenience and a play, not as a reality.

But the Sacred Element work, requiring great self-discipline and self-control, is not the esoteric discovery of the inner self. The esoteric school prepares the initiate. After 'graduation' comes life in the world. The lessons learned in the esoteric school are applied in real life situations. All the preparation was for this very work; it is a work of greatest deepest love.

This must not be misinterpreted as dealing with 'elementals' or earth spirits. The Sacred Element work is more like physics than like astral play, more of a ritual than a control of elemental spirits. It is not spiritualism, nor is it oracular.

The ancient Greek knowledge was all based in the principles of this Symbolical activity. All music, all art form, all geometry, philosophy and science - the concept of man separate from nature, thereby creating nature herself - sprang at heart from Sacred Element symbology. It is the beauty of the balance of the elements.

The moment in history when humanity senses the separation of human life from nature, which we can see as the fall of man, is also the moment of creation of humanity, of creation of nature - a necessary separation which allows greater love. Now history brings humanity full cycle back into the ecology of nature once more, back in the return journey bearing knowledge, and pain of separation. This pain of separation causes tremendous longing, and a great desire for unity once more. Yet the alienation which the separation from nature causes is a far more insistent evolutionary force, which drives humanity to seek feverishly for that unity once more, and to find it in the father/mother God, that which is beyond - or seemingly so.

To know that realization can be achieved by any person anywhere in the world living under any circumstances is a wonderful aspect of the understanding that humanity, though separate from nature, yet has a sublime purpose to fulfill.

The sages have always sought nature for the peaceful life-giving qualities which flow through her. They have found that unity once again with the father/mother God, and there is a supreme understanding of nature and her importance to humanity. These sages have given the world the messages by which to live life, and the secret language of symbols by which to decode the mysteries of life and all the worlds available to humanity.

By emerging from nature, humanity became able to reach a greater akasha. Then, by using knowledge, humanity began to undertake the stewardship of the earth, through agriculture. The ancient schools of agriculture, which have been called maternal cultures, were the keepers of the understandings of the past (not only the former hunting years and ages, but also the former cycles of human life in this and other worlds). The knowledge they kept is ancient and extremely valuable to the forward development of humanity. For we cannot go forward without bringing also the knowledge of the past, as this alone will bring us a cycle of continuity, the full circle of human knowledge. The symbolism used is deep and almost visceral, yet it carries more than the most mathematical abstraction, describing the workings of an elaborate physics.

The Place of Ceremony

Wherever the ceremony is held becomes a womb of all creation

The carved cave has always been there, or somewhere on earth. It is the home of the valley spirit, mother of the ten thousand things mentioned in the Tao Te Ching.

In earlier civilizations, the place of ceremony was often an actual cave, chosen for its symbolical purpose in creation. It is an akasha, a vast protected space through which potential sends out a self-elaborating impulse.

In the honoring of each of the elements, the conductor of the Sacred Element Ritual puts to rest earth, then water, then fire, then air, then ether. They are honored in order that the participants will be free beyond the matter of earthly existence. In loving ritual, the elements intermingle freely, creating ever-new balances and forms. These forms emerge later in human consciousness. At the end of the ceremony, there is gentleness, a purity, an unutterable gratitude. There is sweetness in the heart. It is great, it is pure, it is whole, it is a universal release of love for all humanity.

It is not mythic, nor is it understandable. What occurs is shrouded in darkness, it is actually a *mystery*, and those involved are *mystics*. It is not worded or discussed. It is a *divine presence*.

Let Us Gather Together Again

Let us gather together again to remember our origin, to celebrate the inner lines on which our lives are drawn. And let us remember not by thinking but by repeating again the ancient formula of movement-speech and song.

Like ripples, the waves spread in all directions as the remembrance links with the past to create the future. It has been done so many many times it becomes one thing/one action continuous over all time. This resonant gong must continually be struck by the peoples of the world. If it is not done, then the foundation of creation begins to crumble. Rebuilding requires more effort and is much more difficult than maintenance.

The process of symbology naturally assists the reconstruction. Western society and industrialized nations have worked out the impulse which the last rising of element symbology encouraged. Now comes another rising, another thunder, another striking of the powerful evolutionary impulse. Guided by devoted workers, the resonance will straighten and align all the forces which are now deformed and which have lost touch with their original face. Weak births, natural and unnatural dangers - the problems which conscious working in element symbology will help to solve is a long list of the woes of humanity.

The cure will come by realignment of and with the elements, the basis of our bodies and our minds.

Those involved in this effort vow to help humanity. They sacrifice themselves, to be reworked by God, so that the new flesh, the new mind and emotions can become more and more of service.

Those who can live and observe in both the inner and outer worlds create the ideal on earth.

All Words Concerning Symbology

All words concerning symbology are simply exploratory and are not in any way certain or permanent. A problem of describing this work in words is that it becomes conceptually framed, leading away from its true meaning.

The emotional balance required of initiates is impossible to describe in words. The exploration in this work brings to the surface human intentions, translated personally as feelings and ideas. Behind these personal interpretations, which are both central and peripheral, the human intentions - metahuman, ancient, and destined to fulfillment - surface in order that they may begin again their true force.

All ceremonies aside, it is in the total love of humanity that the Sacred Element ceremonies are acted out, for without this love the understandings are cold and can become calculating. And it is not the love of "God" or "light" or any abstraction. It is pure sweet fierce love of God light as humanity. This means each one is loved totally as God in a particular human form. It is not a separating out, a loving of God and a hating or ignoring of the personality. The whole thing is total, without the personality God would have no means of manifestation, no place in which to work.

The true symbolical working makes this fierce love inevitable. Gratitude overflows. The conductor loves all like a mother loves her variety of children. To those who wish to involve themselves, she gives all she can to encourage and strengthen, so that they too can develop this fierce protective all-encompassing love.

This love springs spontaneously from understanding human nature as it is based in the action and interaction of the elements. It is the celebration of this relationship enacted symbolically in the ceremony which gives to the soul an accurate symbolic picture of its true condition.

A Connected Revival

The symbolical activity is the connected revival of the ancient Greek mystery schools (see below, commentaries on the *Gathas, 5. Oracles among the Ancient Greeks, 6. The Greek Mysteries, 7. The Greek Mysteries (2). 8. The Greek Mysteries (3)*)

The Greater mysteries and the inner initiations correspond to the path which is the Sufism of all ages.

Those who wish to take the Message in a symbolical form discover a history which reveals itself through inner insights, as and when it is needed.

This study heightens all activity of each element in the nature of the initiate. Those involved find their nature shifting and changing more frequently than before, but there is greater awareness and ability to control these shifting moods. These moods are seen as they are, not with emotional identification. And in this way others are also more easily understood. Life is seen as living art, in which balance and equipoise are constantly being sought, found, and transformed again and again.

Human Ecology

The Universal Worship service showers the unified blessings of all masters, saints and prophets (as in the Invocation, in the form of the Spirit of Guidance of all these) through the inner blessing of its sacred directing of symbols and uniting the devotion of the world's great religions. The power and beauty of these forces have created the dynamic civilizations of the world. The Sacred Element work has a similar task, but one which is not as clearly visible.

That task is to unify those impulses which were present as pre-religious dynamic forces. Of course, the religious impulse is common to all humanity in all times. But the pre-religious impulse is that which contains the knowledge of the forces of the manifest and unmanifest world. The wisdom of Solomon and of all the prophets was only this understanding.

The Sacred Element work is a symbolical method of gathering and transmitting this wisdom in the way which is appropriate to these times, when it is needed. The transmitting or expressing occurs simply, almost as an undercurrent or as an overshadowing - in which subtle changes of vibration are made to occur in harmony with those present. This harmony gives to all a remarkable peace in the soul, and a strong sense of basic humanity, with all the exquisite human virtues of love, compassion, gratitude, humility, gentleness, dignity, honor, and many more, including wisdom.

How does this rebalancing occur? Why is it not seen? It requires complete inspiration. The subsequent interpretation of this inspiration in beauty becomes the supreme symbolical representation of the human spirit.

How is this possible? It occurs in a spontaneous way because Inayat Khan has prepared deeply the unseen world for this occurrence. In the Sacred Element work, the potent beauty of the Sufi impulse becomes clear and predominant, with the participants active in developing humanity through self-discipline, love and service.

As to those who dedicate themselves to service through the self-discipline of the love engendered through this work, the transparency of the physical vehicle becomes more and more evident as time goes by. Those involved in Symbolical activity as disincarnate incarnations are transparent vehicles, fully conscious of the simultaneous beauty of both worlds, seen and unseen, inner and outer. They are not a secret priesthood, nor are they a secret society.

The symbols are their own protection, revealing themselves only to those who can comprehend them. The conductor of the ceremonies has a special function and a sacred responsibility. But in no way does this set her/him apart as a special person, someone more than and less than human. No, there is instead an amplification of human virtues and qualities, while progress through the stages of life on earth is made more and more interesting.

Participation in Symbolical activity, in the transforming of all through beautiful recognition, is a demanding lifelong dedication. In its aspect on earth, this effort involves ceremony, training, and art and education for humanity at large. The art and education is specifically tailored for the times in which it is given, with attention to the needs of humanity and the required development. These provide outer mysteries, which cover and uncover themselves.

The understandings and responsibilities given to those entrusted with the work of symbology cannot be put into words. Those offering this service offer all without even knowing what the outcome will be, as through creative perception the world is made new.

To express the Sufi Message through symbology is no greater or lesser than any of the other vehicles established to carry on the Sufi effort in the west. But the way of working in the Sacred Element ceremony requires tremendous subtlety and grace combined with a will of steel, all in a heart of pure golden love. It is a demonstration of humanity. The outpouring of deepest poetry, music, art, and ritual convenes to produce the mystical inner temple in each one.

By insight the history of element symbology is revealed. Naturally it is correspondent to the history of science - an evolution building on the work of previous thinkers, but the vital difference is that this present effort absorbs and synthesizes all that has gone before. That is, it does not discredit or throw out work that is no longer applicable, as in science. Over time, each new wave of symbology is created spontaneously and works with the elements as evolved through previous workers - with all as a total unified synthetic whole.

Humanity: a great experiment evolving God
Sacred Element work: one way of approaching the effort consciously.

Although the ritual ceremony appeals to many, the symbolical work itself appeals to very few. When it begins, the initiate feels 'at last I have found it' but this sense soon erodes, leaving darkest emptiness.

Once the emptiness has turned all into a capacity, the play of the elements begins to be seen. The understanding of life begins also, and the direction of life's purpose is unmistakable., undeniable. The initiate becomes the embodiment of his or her life's purpose. All else is extraneous and soon falls away.

It could be said that the Sacred Element work will develop into a lasting form of the Sufi Message - carrying it through dark times when the worded message could seem old-fashioned to a visually oriented non-print non-linear society. It is natural in mysticism that the literate mind shifts out to make the open mind possible. But negation of the literate mind only does not at all open the total mind, instead we have a more closed system with dogmas held in icons. The open mind is actually balanced, allowing the full resonance of images all play-space and giving mental constructs exposed scaffolding.

It is in caring, in compassion that the open mind is truly seen. For this mind is so open it includes and expresses the depth of the heart also. The error of analysis of mental function is that the heart is rarely included. But the heart is a vital part of all mental functioning - not in the sense of the mind as interpreter of feeling, but more in the idea of the heart as generator of thought.

Feeling, sympathy, loving-kindness, these are the attributes of a thinking person. The total open mind gives rise to sensitivity, to love, to consideration of others. The open mind expresses a loving heart. The grace of God is in the inner voice which expresses this love as a beautiful atmosphere.

Ecological Balance

The temperament, or nature, gives each person his or her basic outlook and basic element balance. Then life experience and interactions cause rises and falls in these balances.

The person who is concerned only with the element balance is working only with the mind and body. There is also a greater balancing. It is essential that the basic balance be maintained not only because this is the optimal natural human condition, but also because at that point the person is able to fulfill life's purpose. The activation of other ecologies begins and the inner dynamic and balance comes into play, with the so-called higher aspects of the element-vibrations (or angels) taking over the play.

As long as the mind and body are out of balance, there is little chance that the greater human virtues will be able to consistently manifest. In such a condition humanity remains at a barely evolved level until individuals take it upon themselves to balance the varied elements consciously. This work of conscious tuning of the vehicle is so deep and reveals all about the nature of life and of the world, it is a life's work in itself.

At each of the stages in a person's life this ecology shifts through great upheavals and rebalances in different order, creating a new condition, requiring other actions on the part of the person to retune the fine instrument again and again. Then there comes a profound change which is irreversible. The ecological balance has been relatively maintained for a period of time long enough that the organism intuitively recognizes the subtle differences and will spontaneously rebalance autonomically. At such a point, training has been completed. Retuning is necessary, but requires little effort and is only a reminder.

It is possible to remain in basic equilibrium under most average conditions. At this time, external life conditions also are in a relatively equal state, and in a cooperative symbiotic harmony with the balanced elements of the human being. Others also sense and respond to this balance, which radiates out a definite positive life signal, and life calls forth from this person all the human qualities which can then be seen fully without impurities on a consistent and continuous basis.

This state is not static, or stiff, but is like a continuous improvised symphony of body, mind, emotions and circumstances which continues throughout life.

At the same time as this balanced ecology is functioning in total harmony, the inner life comes more and more to the threshold of experience until it is one with the outer life and is experienced in the symphonic totality as the melodic theme. When attended to, the theme also reveals a fully glorious silence, from where the person receives great sustenance.

This sustaining presence is translated through the prepared vehicle of the person's body and mind to give sustenance to all of humanity. As this tremendous offering to humanity occurs, the human qualities commingle with qualities evolutionarily seen as 'beyond human'. In this condition, or further stage, the one who undertakes this work is not seen by all as good or virtuous by any means. By this time the general public has no understanding of the dynamic of these translated elements in a transfigured ecology and the manifestation of 'divine' attributes is often misunderstood - either adored as beyond reach or hated by threatened egos.

But the early ecological balance, now autonomic, confers the proper force to each one as required to continue the cohesive flow of conditions necessary for human evolution. And the work becomes more and more inner, using reflection rather than action to accomplish the purpose. By this time, the ecology of the inner life has been similarly balanced, trained and maintained.

This training is not done in the sense of training animals without consideration for the animals' spirit and will; or of cultivating fields without consideration for the intimate relationship of soil and natural plants. All training and maintenance, both inner and outer, retain and encourage joy and life force without stunting the will in any way. For it is the will which carries the symphonic melody.

There is sacrifice, but it is willing sacrifice. There is austerity, but that is to strengthen the will. There is renunciation, but it is only seen as such from without, within it is a celebration.

The balance of a human being - all elements within and without - can be expressed in terms of rhythm and tone and harmony. The vibration of each element causes the moiré patterns of the 3 dimensional energy field or nexus called a human being. At the meeting point of these intense patterns [each with a direction, force, tone, purpose, and dominance) is a vibrant life, all kept in totality and wholeness by the power of the soul, which rules and controls the vibrations for its purpose and fulfillment. These elements create and maintain the vehicle by which the soul experiences life.

A moment of balance gives the soul a rare picture of its true condition and strengthens the will to control the varied elements as they jockey for dominance, each in its own way.

The direct impulse of life force occurs through humanity now as it always has done. However the difference now is that structures and rhythms are developed which direct the intention of this impulse in varied directions, resulting in multiple convolutions and shifts in the actual manifestation of the original impulse. Once the correction of the structures occurs, there regains a balance which is not ever possible when the structures remain as they are now. Presently they divert and diffuse the original life force and often contort it beyond recognition, away from its original objective.

This situation must be acknowledged and understood as a dreadful warning that humanity cries out to become mature, that the present pitiful idea of education does nothing for the heart or the will or the integrity, and the understanding of the noble dignity of humanity must be spread to all.

The 'types' of the 'perfect forms' can impress themselves once again as they did of old on the very heart of matter in its organization, and they will be seed crystals, as it were, to the evolving world - with an incidental catalytic effect, which is profound and recognizable. The effect involves a real change in social, economic, and physical structures of society (as in the Renaissance and any other major shift). When change is about to occur, element symbology is a necessary regulator. Once the mechanical action of phenomena occurs, there is no turning back or stopping it, only a harmonization of tone and rhythm until the new influence is felt by the mechanism, gradually more and more in its power.

Such work is not to be taken lightly as it requires dedication, determination, strength, will, compassion, love and integrity. It develops the noble human being one little step closer to full manifestation, and it adds another voice to the many who have gone before in evolving the world.

It could be said that the life's work of any individual is preparing the capacity in which to do that life's work. Few are 'born into' the ideal situation which will give the purpose of life all it needs. Usually, the soul must get down into the muck of it all, to actively create the conditions according to its requirements before beginning what it was destined to do.

The soul may have to change the lives of those around it, solving problems and creating a happier atmosphere. It may have to physically change environments in order to feel a sense of peace, or even to wage war or defend the country of its birth before engaging in its true purpose on earth. Or it may have to feed those around it, or transform laws, or arts, or science. All the while, the soul is creating the capacity in which to engage in its purpose toward fulfillment.

Service is therefore not intentional, yet it is necessary and the sign of the saintly. For a great soul to fulfill its purpose, service to humanity is the only way to relieve its own suffering, and without that relief, there can be no life fulfillment. Great souls born into immature humanity first must help others - but still keep sights on the purpose of life.

Thus it is that few souls indeed can fulfill this destiny on earth, and those who do are ranked among great beings, considered remarkable or holy ones. Yet in truth these persons are only being naturally human, claiming their birthrights. Like stars, they burn very brightly to illuminate the night.

The effect of Sacred Element concentration is light and the tendency to always help others sense that light. It is not heavy or pious, or pretentiously over-serious.

The secret of life on earth is translated into the 5 elements and their play. The intellectual scaffolding of these concepts has been in place throughout all of western and eastern civilization, but it has been neglected in recent years.

Color, art, symbology, the laws of vibrations, all have their root in awareness and understanding of the play of the elements. The deck of cards with 4 suits, the Tarot Major Arcana being ether the 5th element, indicate this teaching. All alchemy, all science and astrology use this cultural scaffolding. In the idea of the resurgence of Sacred Element ceremonies as a cultural phenomenon in present times is the ecstasy of unity of elements which will begin to show itself as a possible reality. This effort does not grow quickly; at least the understanding of it, for it requires an intense involvement on the part of the initiate - an involvement which most people are uninterested in pursuing.

But for those who do have the aspiration, the Sufi Message of Inayat Khan offers this capacity in which to learn and play. It is a learning which comes as austerities and self-discipline. The play is the natural play of the universe: to be an active participant in this play is the goal of the initiate. It is an ecstasy so refined. And to be ready to experience this, it is the initiate who is refined again and again through the active working of the elements in the ecology of human life and nature.

The interdependency of the continual balancing of elements has often caused the initiate to appear in symbolism as a juggler. For it is active working with the elements which gives the initiate experiences which accumulate to become the refining process. It is not a sudden overnight occurrence. To be fine and strong as steel wire is no small feat. And then to walk unassisted along that self-created wire is an act of human daring.

Symbology is a circus, it is a school of agriculture, it is present day alchemy, it is human ecology. Ultimately all ideas, metaphors, and symbols fade. Human life becomes expressive of the divine in magnetic purity. Evolution is assisted.

The mystery itself fades in the magnitude of the ONLY BEING. Then the goal of all universal play is achieved as divine ecstatic delight. The joy of Symbology is the privilege of participation.

Training, Ceremony, Art and Education

Symbolical activity appears to be divided into three main aspects: the training (which is inner), the ceremony, and art and education (outer and for humanity at large).

The training is an inner growth involving a greater understanding of human ecology using the breath, other indicators of the elements, and inner initiations.

The ceremony is a celebration and a service, a play of death, a devotion, a ritual.

The Art and Education aspect is the outer gift to society at large.

These three aspects are interdependent and often simultaneous. They are all both inner and outer at the same time as well. Thus the training is not only inner work, but involves the total environment of the adept as well as the inner centres.

Everything is always seen and known in relation, in context, as interactive and interdependent. Nature, or human nature, is studied both within and without, and 'the universe in man' becomes more and more visible as a living reality.

Identification and analysis give way to synthesis.

Poetically, the human being is described and known to contain and express all things, all elements, all of nature and what appears beyond earthly nature. All animals, all weathers and climates, all varieties of vegetation, all forms of fruit and flower, all types of terrain and water formations are seen in humanity. All angelic qualities, all powers of mind, all virtues and aspirations, all capabilities for tremendous evil, all good and wisdom - it is there in the human capacity. Looking outward, we see the picture of humanity as the world, looking within; we see the universe in ourselves. It is one life.

Symbology reveals life, unveiling the secret of the pine tree, the meaning of tears. It shows the stars of the intellect, the fire of the heart, the supreme elegance of grace and gratitude. In Symbology, the Sufi Message is known, seen, felt and heard in and through all things, events, and circumstances, but most especially in all beings. In a most natural way, Symbology reveals the innermost secret of humanity simply and without pretense.

The Sacred Element ceremony exemplifies and deepens the Sufi thought that there is one holy book, the sacred manuscript of nature, and the idea that nature is the only teacher. Of course, our present idea of nature, and of what nature is, is limited by the earth element, for just as the breakthrough came into ecological understanding, so our idea of nature must break to include (re-include again) ourselves: humanity, inextricably and totally involved in nature's cycles. As this effort is the worship of God in human nature, the elements and their play only offer a helpful vocabulary. Understanding the elements is not the focus. It is the understanding and refinement of human nature which is involved, not the abstraction of element, color, direction, etc.

These ideas can be seen and known and as they come to form in the consciousness of the adept, the vocabulary of the elements gives a great richness and appreciation to life. Just as in music, it can be felt and understood on various levels. One unschooled in music may feel and understand its communication heart to heart, while another technician may be so involved analyzing the musical form and performance that the intent and contact of the music are lost. Better yet, to experience music from the point of view of a composer requires technique, appreciation, skill in expression and inspiration. Then is expressed the song of the soul.

Just so in life: the art of personality reaches its peak in the human being who is a composer of life, using the elements in beautiful control to express this art of life - or is it allowing the elements play through disciplined improvisation?

The Symbolical Activity is not simply the study of the interaction of the elements. That is only a useful alphabet, a stimulus to understanding. The action of this study helps open the adept to the perception of the presence of God in humanity, as humanity, and all. There is little worth in the analysis of all things as earth, water, fire, air, and ether [and even the subtle analysis of the breath] without the inner perception of the divine ideal.

On earth, in manifestation, love, lover and beloved are caught in their own web. The web of perceptions elaborated by thought can never penetrate itself to become pure insight. Insight, intuition, wisdom, all come from within, from beyond the web. It is only from such a viewpoint that the alphabet of the elements can be effectively known and understood - as a help to understanding life and humanity - as an aid to synthesis rather than analysis.

The love of humanity, the service of God through man, the gentleness of purity, do not need analysis of the elements. The understanding of symbols is awakened spontaneously, without analysis of the elements. The Message itself is passed from person to person without analysis of the elements. Subtlety is the most necessary attribute of mind when dealing with these questions.

Of course, the heritage of ancient wisdom has always included the basic understanding of the elements, their attributes and their manifestation.

In healing body and mind, in everyday life, in controlling or mastering circumstances, the applied knowledge of the elements has proven invaluable down through the ages. In our times there is not much difference, for an understanding of the action of the elements helps in our understanding of life and ourselves. But to develop this awareness fully, it must, paradoxically, be abandoned. In the Sacred Element ceremony, each element is honored, but what is left is exalted humanity - each human being as a unique beautiful manifestation of God.

From the Sufi Message of Inayat Khan

The Sufi Message of Inayat Khan, volumes and esoteric papers, contain much information concerning this effort, which can help a great deal in understanding this way of working. I have selected some excerpts (in italics) and provided commentaries (in plain type) which may be helpful in expanding these powerful seed-ideas which Inayat Khan left with us for our furthering of this work.

On The Ancient Greek Mysteries
(from Gatha II)

Oracles Among the Ancient Greeks

In ancient Greece often questions were asked of an oracle, which were answered by a woman, who sometimes gave a plain answer and some times one the meaning of which was veiled.

The woman "channeled" the oracular answers, whether openly or with a more mystical meaning. It was as if the woman did not exist, except in her function of speaking the oracle. It was the oracle who veiled or opened the answer.

It was the same thing that today is called a spiritualistic séance, a mediumistic answer, the interest of which is alive in all ages though in different forms.

The gods spoke through the woman as spirits through a medium, giving the answers the inquirers dared not see for themselves. In all times humanity has been fascinated with this phenomenon of "obsession" or "possession" of a human being by a super-human force or entity.

Among all occult and mystical interests, the interest in the medium has a very great attraction for the average mind.

To the Sufi or mystic this type of thing is not so mysterious or interesting, but to an average person the mediumistic trance is a compelling proof that there is more to life than meets the eye.

A woman was often chosen for this work, on account of woman's sensitiveness, which always exceeds that of man, and this is the secret of intuition in human nature.

Most often, women priestesses or oracles were chosen, and trained in this pure intuitive work. The receptive sensitivity opens completely to the other side and inner worlds, while the masculine creative aspect is more closed to these realms and must be induced to sensitivity by love or pain. Women with enhanced femininity and receptivity are naturally sensitized. The development of intuition in both men and women requires receptivity and sensitivity.

Especially a celibate woman was chosen for this purpose, as in her is to be found more susceptibility to intuition.

The intuition and openness of inner centres is increased by continence and the clear emptiness of the celibate woman becomes a living womb for intuitive force and vibrant receptive energy. When the energy is being continuously balanced by the earth (through man and lovemaking) there may not be as strong a call to God. When the energy is balanced by heaven, the celibate woman becomes a ringing bell with a clear strong tone. However, life on earth in such a state of sensitivity is too difficult, which is why the oracle is protected and cloistered by the priests.

The question was supposed to be asked of a god, a god who was distinguished by a particular attribute, of poetry, of the sun or any other attribute.

The woman becomes easily able to reflect the impression (in the intuition) of this god, and to channel and reflect both question and response. This god believed in by the Greeks would then "speak through" the woman who was sensitized and trained to do this.

The secret of all this is that the priests, by their hypnotic power and suggestion, wakened in the woman that particular attribute of the Spirit within, Who is the possessor of all knowledge, especially that pertaining to the attribute with which He is identified.

The oracle was trained esoterically by the priests, who inculcated in her the ability to resonate the particular interest or attribute of the god. They would train the oracle with great delicacy, for fear of blunting her sensitivity. Yet at the same time, their duty was to impress upon her the direction in which her intuitive responsiveness was to be concentrated.

They would then mould or create in the space or womb of her intuition the being of God - using only the attributes of the all-pervading Spirit which they were most familiar with. It was a holy, esoteric (bodiless) lovemaking and impregnation of the highest purity.

God is already in the heart of every person, only to wake Him and make Him rise, He should be called upon.

The power of this esoteric training comes not from the egos or the dogmas of those involved, but from God within, latent, available if only called and awakened. The priests wakened the God within the oracle woman by means of their holy devotion and the God in their hearts wakened the God in her heart, in response. Then the devotion became a reality and they worshipped the god they had helped to 'create'.

He then, so to speak, takes birth from the heart of a sensitive woman, whose innermost can easily be touched.

By such training, by being heightened in sensitivity, by abstinence and fasting, by being placed in states of consciousness and given repeated suggestions, the woman prepared for this virgin birth which occurred spontaneously. From this time forward, they dwelled together, the woman and the god, interpenetrated. But as this situation is specialized and tuned specifically for one purpose only, the oracle was treated with great care and protection by the priests.

God has many attributes, He has many ears and tongues to speak with, and through every form He answers whenever one reaches Him.

This specialized Greek oracle is not the only one with the ability to reflect the attributes of God. At any time, in any place, any person could actively reflect this divinity. Any object, any living thing, all are the power of God and manifestations of God's multiplicity of attributes. Therefore, one can reach God here and now, not only through the specialized intensity of the oracle.

Spiritualists call Him a spirit, but even through the spirit of an individual, dead or living, when God is called upon, God answers.

It is the One God who is behind all mediumistic expressions and those which are not. To God goes all love and gratitude, not to the limited individuals or particular attributes which reflect a part of the enormous reality of the Being of God.

Those who play with spiritualistic séances would give it all up in a moment if they only knew that God always answers whenever He is called upon.

Here Inayat Khan delivers the punch line - it is not necessary to consult mediums and oracles when God is ever-present, ready to respond if only asked.

The Symbology has no particular connection with the oracular line, but spreads humanly in all directions, seeing, knowing, and reflecting God in all things and all beings.

The Greek Mysteries (1)

The little that is known of the Greek Mysteries has been very variously interpreted.

We have fragments of (outer) information concerning just what these mysteries were, and over the centuries, historians, scholars and occultists have hazarded interpretations concerning these events.

Some have supposed them to have been a course of agriculture, taught secretly, others a mummery carried on for centuries by the priests.

Here Inayat Khan gives the Sufi view and the hint of the Symbology in the code "a course of agriculture, taught secretly". The mummery, or ancient theatrical presentation ritual was also part but was more exoteric. The school of agriculture was given to people the world over in the great transition to agrarian herding life from hunting and gathering. It is a secret initiatory program preparing humanity for the evolutionary step, and teaches humankind how to evolve further.

What is known with certainty is the high esteem in which they were held and the strict secrecy which attended them.

The mysteries were the highest knowledge. Those participating were as Gods. There was no leak of information to non-initiates, all initiates were silent. It was never defiled in that sense, and the symbols retained power for centuries as a result.

The word means silence: to be initiated was 'to be made silent'.

All worldly secret societies imitate this rule, which was no doubt essential. Perhaps humanity was so stratified that all those who could know, did know (like the Brahmin caste in India), and the others simply could not have translated the information if they had heard it. It is possible that mystery experiences were untranslatable even to the initiates, thereby ensuring secrecy and silence by the nature of the experience.

Access to the lesser mysteries was easy.

People in multitudes were given the everyday instruction, much like our churches, but with oracle consultation, dramatic presentations, and great emphasis on superstition and taboo. It kept the populace busy, educated those who were interested, deflected attention away from the inner mysteries.

Tens of thousands were initiated.

Those with a religious bent were initiated and satisfied with the stage of instruction given, which was only a shadow of the inner school.

The temples in which the rites were practiced were under the protection of the state.

It was the national expression of religious feeling, the common way for all. It was socially and politically cohesive and sustaining to the state and the group consciousness of the people.

In them were enacted the lives of the gods in whose name the mysteries were celebrated, and great use was made of music.

These were the mummeries, symbolic enactments to instruct the people. Music tuned the soul, and the emotions were released and purified.

The mysteries were held to remove the fear of death and to give assurance of survival of the departed.

The symbolic enactments, coupled with music, were repeated seasonally throughout life. This impression accumulated, to instruct and reassure people.

Those who had been initiated were believed to be happy after death, while others led a dismal life hereafter, clinging to their graves.

The dogma of the state religion reinforced popular cohesion with the status quo, rendering a stable society.

The preparatory training for the greater mysteries was very severe.
 Mere curiosity seekers were discouraged from participating in the greater mysteries by rigorous training which separated out those who were not strong enough mentally, physically and emotionally.

Fasting was undergone, abstinence of all sorts, extremes of heat and cold had to be endured, and the candidates swam through water for days and had to walk through fire.
 Aside from all physical trainings, the emotional training was undergone with the assistance of the elements. This was not simply training as in the physical army sense. It was a training involving the overwhelming of the elements and the inner strength to overcome their influence.

The training often lasted many years.
 Under the protection of the initiates, candidates were placed in circumstances of great difficulty for years. They were tested by earth, water, fire and air. They were given particular training of the will.

After initiation, in the beginning, all was darkness, dread and dismay; then a marvelous light was seen and shining forms came to meet the initiate.
 This simulation of death, or experience of 'death', was central to the initiatory process.

The initiate experienced while on earth the state of the soul dissociated from the body.
 All the training was to ensure safe passage, to ensure that the initiate had the will and control to sustain such a holy act as death before physical death. Disincarnate incarnation. Die before death. It is Sufi training. The initiate in this condition is free, and all knowledge is self-revealing.

Apuleuis, who had received all the initiations of the mysteries, says, "I went to the boundary between life and death, I passed through the four elements, I stood on the threshold of Proserpina, at the time of deepest midnight I saw the sun shine in brightest splendor, I saw the greater and the lesser gods and revered them near at hand."

> Here Inayat gives the stages of mystical initiations:
1. The boundary between life and death (esoteric school)
2. The four elements - earth, water, fire, air. (symbology)
3. The threshold of Proserpina (ether)
4. Deepest darkness yields brilliant light (inner initiation)
5. At one with the gods (inner initiation)

The initiate was said to be received, while living on earth, among the immortal gods, and made one with them.

The sequence of initiation is vitally important, for those involved in the mysteries were taken through the correct series of steps to ensure total safety. There could be no arrogance, no 'left hand path' due to the very severity of the training and initiations. The mysteries could never be expressed. The secret, though openly stated, remains well guarded.

The Greek Mysteries (2)

This was really a Sufi institution, though not called by this name, for exactly the same thing is to be found today in the schools of Sufis in India and Persia.

Here Inayat Khan tells the source of his direct information on the mysteries, with the lineage traced back from Sufis into ancient Greece and deeper still. It is clear that he reveals that the thread is present in his teaching today but not at this point revealed.

The lesser mysteries were Ilmi Rabbali, the mystery of the gods, in other words the mystery of the different attributes of God.

Here he translates the Greek Lesser Mysteries as they were to the Sufi version, the wazifas or more clearly, the esoteric school of Sufism with the uses of vibration, sound, esoteric breath, etc. His vast awareness is made clear by the way he sees the Greek Lesser Mysteries in essence, and that essence as culturally translated in Sufi lore.

For when the proper name of God is repeated a certain number of times some particular effect is produced by it, resulting in a desirable object.

This is the mysticism of sound and vibration.

Before Islam the different names of God were considered to be different gods known by different names and identified with different attributes and characteristics.

Islam means peace, surrender, and symbolizes unity for all 'gods', united as one God with many attributes.

By invoking the names of different gods a person accomplished his object in life, as now Wazifa is practiced by the Sufis.

These are still the lesser mysteries. He proves here that the gods were used by the Greeks just as the attributes are used by Sufis.

The music which the ancient Greek knowers of mystery had as a means of spiritual development, the same is used even now in the Chistia schools of Sufis, where the Qawwali meeting which is called Sama, is held in which music is played and sung for awakening the emotional nature, which is the secret of revelation.

The formulae of Greek mystery music are kept and transmitted in Sufi music forms to stimulate and expand the emotions and spirit. This form of listening in holiness, of performing sacred formulae is still the same in present Sufi gatherings.

The Greek Mysteries (3)

The fasting and abstinence, and all these things, were taught in order to develop the will-power, which results in self-discipline and which is the secret of all mastery; and it is by this power that the kingdom within is attained.

The training includes abstinence and fasting to develop the will, along with other renunciations, deprivations, etc. All these methods are not ends in themselves but are employed as tools to uncover and strengthen the will. Developed will power shows in self-mastery, not in the mastery of others. It gives a self-discipline to the life of the initiate which will ensure safety in all realms. With will-power, the self-disciplined person becomes master of all. The inner kingdom is open to that one and life is a rich reality.

Once a man has touched his self within, the illusion becomes dissolved.

The inner reality of the kingdom within opens to the one trained in self-mastery and self-discipline. At this opening, all is truth. There is no longer any falsehood. Truth is all, there is not even any illusion.

The fear of death is caused by the consciousness of mortality.

The line between life and death is maintained by fear. The mastered self sees this line as illusion and dissolves it. Being conscious beyond mortality, man has no fear of death, but sees it as it is.

As long as one is unaware of one's immortal self one has the fear of death.

Fear of death and fear of one's immortal self are very much alike and the same. Death is no longer death when one is aware of and one with one's immortal self. To embrace and become the immortal self is to embrace death and become free of the illusion of fear.

Once immortality of the soul is realized and the realization is no longer in one's imagination but has become a conviction, then one rises above the fear of death.

The imagined realization is the lesser mystery. A step toward the goal, it is believed but has yet to be experienced. The true realization of immortality has no space for fear of death, only beauty and life and truth. It is not known, but only is.

This knowledge is gained fully when the adept is able to detach his soul from his body. It is this state which is called by Yogis Samadhi and by Sufis Nayat.

When consciousness fully resides not in the mind/body but in the soul itself, all knowledge of life and death becomes clear.

Every soul that treads the path of initiation takes his first steps through the darkness; as Ghazzali says, "The spiritual pursuit is like shooting an arrow through darkness."

At the beginning of this shift of consciousness from body/mind to soul, it is confusing, dark and chaotic. A person isn't sure what is going on at all and must have faith that the arrow shot out into complete darkness will after all reach its mark.

No doubt as one approaches the goal, the light comes; as the Koran says, "God is the light of the heavens and the earth."

As the initiate proceeds as or in the soul, light comes from God to meet the soul.

This light shines to illuminate not only the heavens but also things on earth are illuminated as well. This illumination is one with understanding.

Then, once the sight has become keen, there is no further instruction needed. This light illuminates the soul's path until the soul unites with it and becomes its own illumination. No other instruction is needed, for the illumination within and without reveals all things.

One gets insight into the hidden laws of nature, all things seem to speak to the seer of their character, nature and secret.

These insights are clear and spontaneous, untaught, direct percepts.

This realization removes the boundary between life and death.

Once the soul is fully functioning simultaneously in all realms, there is not a strict separation called "life" or "death" but only one life in immortality.

One rises above the elements which have formed this mortal abode - the body and mind - for the soul's experience, when one touches one's true being, the soul.

The elements earth, water, fire, and air, form the body and mind in which the soul is captive upon birth in human form. The soul identifies with these elements as the vehicle of its experience. The initiate rises above this vehicle and experiences life through the soul rather than through the mind and body.

It is the soul-realized man who stands above all matter, and in this way the spirit gets victory over matter.

The individual initiate who overcomes matter, and experiences immortal life as a soul, stands in command of the elements. The initiate at that point represents all humanity, enacting the ancient age-old struggle of spirit and matter. By control of will, the initiate develops mastery, which overcomes the influences of the elements within him/herself. Spirit is victorious after death, but the initiate dies before death in order to live as a soul now.

Under all conditions of life which produce obscurity and confusion, the soul-realized man sees the light, and to him all men, of lesser or greater degrees of evolution, are nothing but different forms of the Divine immanence.

In the conditions of life, the adept sees the play of the elements as the worship of God. He loves all beings as expressions of God. Life is a divine symphonic play or ritual in which all parts are performed by aspects of One Being.

In this way, the man who has probed the depth of the mystery of life becomes God-realized.

By taking the path of the Mysteries, the initiate goes through intensities and levels of experience and initiation which heighten the awareness and strengthen the will and self-discipline. The mastery of self so gained will allow him/her to pass the threshold of life and death to live as a soul-realized one. The point of view of the soul is the next step to God-realization.

When he no longer has his limited self before his view then only he experiences the state of which Christ has spoken: "Be ye perfect as your Father in heaven is perfect."

Christ was an initiate who promised to show to others the way to the perfection of soul-realization. The words cannot convey the meaning of the mystery schools and their far-reaching work, which is why symbology is used.

From A Message of Spiritual Liberty
(Volume 5 Sufi Message Volumes)

All planes of existence consist of vibrations...the vibrations of each plane have come from a higher one and have become grosser. Whoever knows the mystery of vibrations, indeed knows all things. Vibrations are of 5 different aspects, appearing as the five elements:
1. Nur - ether
2. Baad - air
3. Atesh - fire
4. Aab - water
5. Khaak - earth
(p.26)

Groups of Five

I assume that whenever Inayat Khan expresses groups of five, or organizes his thoughts in groups of five, he refers to their vibrational relationship, and that this corresponds to the action of the various elements as vibration patterns. Like modern physics, it is a relative phenomenon, so what is earth in relation to water in one situation may act as water in relation to fire in another, etc.

Planes

1. Hahut - plane of consciousness   [ether]
2. Lahut - spiritual plane   [air]
3. Jabarut - astral plane   [fire]
4. Malakut - mental plane   [water]
5. Nasut - material plane   [earth]
(p.25)

Stages of Consciousness

1. Nabi - prophet   [ether]
2. Qutb - saint   [air]
3. Wali - holy man   [fire]
4. Insan - wise man   [water]
5. Adam - ordinary man   [earth]
(p.25)

Five Natures
1. Salima - one who sacrifices for the benefit of others — [ether]
2. Alima - one who thinks, speaks and acts right — [air]
3. Mutmaina - one who considers before taking action — [fire]
4. Lauwama - one who repents of his follies — [water]
5. Ammara - one who acts under the influence of the senses — [earth]

(p.25)

The descriptions of the types may not seem to represent the attitude of that element, for example, the one who considers before taking action does not seem to have the qualities of 'fire', yet in the context of the analysis of the five natures, this attribute is in that place of 'fire' in the progressive vibration scale.

Dreams
1. Khayali - actions and thoughts of the day are reproduced in sleep [earth]
2. Qalbi - dream is opposite to the real happening [water]
3. Naqshi - real meaning is disguised by a symbolic representation which only the wise can understand [fire]
4. Ruhi - real happening is literally shown [air]
5. Elhami - divine messages are given in letters or by an angelic voice. [ether] (p.29)

Types of Inspiration
1. Elham-e-Ilm - inspiration of an artist and scientist — [earth]
2. Elham-e-Husn - inspiration of a musician and poet — [water]
3. Elham-e-Ishq - inspiration of a devotee — [fire]
4. Elham-e-Ruh - inspiration of a mystic — [air]
5. Elham-e-Ghayb - inspiration of a prophet — [ether]

(p.30)

Reflection of Inspiration
"Inspirations are reflected upon mankind in five ways:"
1. Kushad der Khyal - in the wave of thought — [earth]
2. Kushad der Ital - in emotions and feelings — [water]
3. Kushad der Jemal - in the sufferings of the heart — [fire]
4. Kushad der Jelal - in the flow of wisdom — [air]
5. Kushad der Kemal - in the divine voice and vision — [ether]

(p.30)

Music has 5 aspects
1. Tarab (artistic) - music which induces motion of the body   [earth]
2. Raga (scientific) - music which appeals to the intellect   [water]
3. Qul (emotional) - music which creates feelings   [fire]
4. Nida (inspirational) - music which is heard in vision   [air]
5. Saut (celestial) - music which is in the abstract   [ether]
(p.31-32)

Ecstasy (Wajad)
1. Ecstasy of dervishes - produces a rhythmic motion of the body
 [earth]
2. Ecstasy of idealists - expressed by a thrilling sensation in the body, tears and sighs   [water]
3. Ecstasy of devotees - creates an exalted state in the physical and mental body.   [fire]
4. Ecstasy of saints - creates perfect calm and peace
 [air]
5. Ecstasy of prophets - realization of the highest consciousness
 [ether]

These descriptions refer to the subtle aspects of the elements as the inner vibratory pattern of all existence even beyond the earth plane. The reference is not to the element as we perceive it in its everyday activity, but rather from a mystical point of view, as the subtle aspects of breath and as a governing pattern or scale of universal activity of the presence of God in less obvious and more subtle manifestation. There is still manifestation, but it is not on the earth plane, it is in the subtle atoms of the breath, in the thought and feeling, and in many other realms not open to the earth plane.

The elements in relation to everyday life
"In relation to these elements, mankind has five senses"
1. Sight - eyes   [ether]
2. Hearing - ears   [air]
3. Smell - nose   [fire]
4. Taste - tongue   [water]
5. Touch - skin   [earth]

(p.26, also p.231, Metaphysics) However, the great subtlety of hearing could indicate that ether should be related to hearing rather than sight.

This categorization, however, does not refer to body parts, but to the functioning of the senses through their organ of perception. The body itself is categorized differently in functioning, as below.

Body Functioning

1. Skin, flesh, bones -	[earth]
2. Blood, perspiration, saliva -	[water]
3. Heat and digestion -	[fire]
4. Breath and movement -	[air]
5. Controls activities, gradually consumes all other elements -	[ether]

(Metaphysics, p.229)

And the body is categorized differently again when the parts themselves represent the elements.

Body Parts
1. Earth - bones
2. Water - flesh
3. Fire - blood
4. Air - skin
5. Ether - hair

(Metaphysics, p.230)

Other groupings include:

Outlet of Refuse
1. Earth - excretion
2. Water - urination
3. Fire - perspiration
4. Air - saliva
5. Ether - semen

(Metaphysics, p.230)

Bodily Desires
1. Earth - motion
2. Water - urination
3. Fire - thirst
4. Air - appetite
5. Ether - passion

(Metaphysics, p.233)

EMOTIONS
1. Earth - fear [with light becomes caution]
2. Water - affection [with light becomes benevolence]
3. Fire - anger [with light becomes ardour]
4. Air - humour [with light becomes joy]
5. Ether - sadness [with light becomes peace]
    (Metaphysics, p.234)

"Whichever element predominates in a person's nature, the sense relative to that is most active. And as the breath changes so many times through the day and night, its element acts in accordance with the senses. This is the cause of every demand of the senses."   (Metaphysics, p.232)

FIVE FACULTIES
1. Ego - identifying   [earth]
2. Reason - memory   [water]
3. Memory - consciousness   [fire]
4. Mind - thinking   [air]
5. Heart - feeling   [ether]

EMOTIONS EXPERIENCED THROUGH THE HEART
Humor [air], Joy [ether], Sorrow [earth], Fear [ether and air], Pity [water], Courage [fire and air], Indifference [ether, fire and air], Passion [fire], Anger [fire and air].
(p.26, also p.231, metaphysics)

THE EGO IN CONNECTION WITH CONSCIOUSNESS
The ego in connection with consciousness can resemble any of the five elements in this way:
1. Earth - like rocks, the lowest form of life, the ego can be stiff, hard, unmovable and unbendable.
2. Water - or the ego can be pliable, serviceable. Like water, it can be poured, can be diverted.
3. Fire - still more pliable, it can be taken from the rock or from the atmosphere, Because it is even more pliable it is much more serviceable.
4. Air - is still more pliable, it is everywhere and man cannot live without it. Such a one becomes indispensable to the universe as is air.
5. Ether - is nearest to us, for it surrounds us and is within us. One whose

ego in connection with consciousness is like the ether is a completely God-realized being.
(Vol.5, Pearls.p.195)

The Five Things Man Yearns For

1. Life   [earth]
2. Power   [water]
3. Knowledge   [fire]
4. Happiness   [air]
5. Peace   [ether]

(Vol.4, Alchemy of Happiness)

There are many other "groups of five" to be found in the books and papers of Inayat Khan which can be examined in the light of the categories of the elements, some explicitly stated as element relationships, others inferred. The Rasa Shastra, for example catalogues "types of lovers".

Combined Attributes

Simply as an exercise, I combined the attributes listed above to create examples of human personalities.

EARTH

Adam, the ordinary man on the material plane, acts under the influence of the senses. The sense of touch, through the skin, is predominant. In dreams, the actions and thoughts of the day are reproduced in sleep. His inspiration is that of the artist and scientist, and is reflected in the wave of thought. He prefers the music which is artistic, which induces motion of the body, and in ecstasy experiences also rhythmic motion of the body. The predominant emotion is fear and caution, he is stiff, hard, immovable, unbendable. Earth functions through the skin, flesh and bones. It is represented by bones, and in the body's desires as motion and excretion. It is connected with the ego which identifies things. A person in the vibration of earth yearns for life.

WATER

The wise man, Insan, lives on the mental plane. He repents of his follies, and his dream is the opposite to the real happening of the day. His inspiration is that of the musician and poet, and this is reflected through the emotions and feelings. He prefers scientific music which appeals to the intellect, and his ecstasy is expressed by a thrilling sensation in the body, by tears and sighs. His sense of taste through the tongue is most predominant, with affection and benevolence as predominant emotions. Water works through the body as blood, perspiration and saliva, and is most represented by the flesh, with urination as the indicative bodily desire. In faculties, water holds memory through reason. A watery nature is pliable, and serviceable. It is useful, and can be diverted, poured and changed. A person in the vibration of water yearns for power.

FIRE
The Wali is a holy man who lives in the astral plane. He is one who considers before taking action. In his dreams, the real meaning is disguised by a symbolic representation which only the wise can understand. His inspiration is that of the devotee and is reflected in the sufferings of the heart. He is attracted to emotional music which creates feelings. His ecstasy is that of devotees, and it creates an exalted state in the physical and mental body. The faculty of memory creates consciousness, primary is the sense of smell through the nose, with heat and digestion reflecting the work of fire in the body. This fire is represented by the blood and manifests as perspiration and thirst. Its primary emotion is anger or ardour. This nature is very useful and serviceable, extremely pliable and easily changed. A person in the vibration of fire yearns for knowledge.

AIR
The qutb or saint lives in the spiritual plane. He is one who thinks and acts right. In his dream, the real happening is literally shown and his inspiration is that of the mystic. This is reflected in the flow of wisdom. He is attracted to the music which is inspirational, and heard in vision. His ecstasy creates perfect calm and peace. His principle emotions are humor and joy and the faculty of mind encourages thinking. Air is seen in the body as breath and movement, and is represented by skin. Saliva and appetite show its effects. Air is extremely useful and changeable. Reflected in the sense of hearing, it is everywhere and man cannot live without it. Similarly, such a person is everywhere, and humanity cannot live without him. A person in the vibration of air yearns for happiness.

ETHER

The Nabi or prophet is in the plane of consciousness. He is one who sacrifices for the benefit of others. To him divine messages are given in letter or by an angelic voice. His inspiration is that of the prophet which comes as a divine voice and vision. His music is heard in the abstract and is celestial. His ecstasy is the realization of the highest consciousness. Ether predominates as the sense of sight through the eyes, and in the body it controls all activities, gradually consuming the others. It is seen as hair, felt as passion, released as semen, and its emotion is sadness or peace. It is shown in the heart faculty and in the capacity of feeling. It is the most useful and fluent of all elements, nearest to us, surrounding us and within us. Such a nature yearns for peace and fully developed, is peace.

Actually all the planes of existence are represented in each human being, for the whole of each element is contained and represented in each human body. Thus we all have within us the capacity to develop into the supreme human being, and become perfect (as Christ said: "Be ye perfect, as your Father in heaven is perfect.") Although each of us has a predominance of one or the other in our nature, through character development the elements can be balanced.

When development of personality unifies the being, the divine spirit conquers matter. This experience is beautifully symbolized in the symbology ceremony, as each element is respected, separated out in turn, leaving only the purity of the divine soul delighting in the display of their play.

Elementary School
Back to the alphabet

From Gathas on breath

In every direction the breath does a special work. The breath has a special work with every organ of the body, and it has a particular influence upon every element of which the physical body consists.
(Gathas, p.135)
There are five centres in the body of man. The breath has its particular work in every centre.
(Gathas, p.136)

From Five Aspects of Breath (Gathas on Breath)

The mechanism of the body is dependent in its work upon five different aspects of breath, and these aspects are the five different directions of breath.

Here Inayat Khan outlines the subject - the relationship of the working of the body and the elements. Seen as five aspects of breath, they are subtly defined in terms of direction, which can be sensed and used consciously.

In the Koran, and also in the Hebrew scriptures, these five breaths are known as the five angels.

The prana is a capacity which accommodates the five varied vibrational spheres. These can be called 'breaths', 'elements' or 'angels'.

These aspects are thus pictured in their finer work in human life.

In their finer work, the elements are seen as angels, beyond the limitations of everyday humanity.

Often their direction is spoken of by the prophets in symbolical terms, as it is said: one stands on the left side of man, one on the right, one before, one behind, one within him.

As well as being conceived of as angels, these elements are seen in direct relation to human beings. Seeing a person standing naturally, the attributes of the angels are shown in the direction of the elements as left, right, forward, behind, and within.

When one aspect of these five is not working properly, it brings disorder in the whole mechanism of the body.

These elements work in harmony with one another and it is their disequilibrium which brings about disease. So the directions of breath must be in their proper places according to their own rhythms.

In eating and drinking, yawning and stretching, and in all actions of everyday life these five aspects of breath have to take the lead.

All movement and desire in the body stems from the elements at play, creating and recreating new harmonies and balances by the change of breath.

Among these five aspects the first is the breath which is like the stem on the tree, and which one feels through the nostrils.

The first breath is the physical breath which leads to the other more subtle breaths. It is the basis, and is central, like the stem of the Tree of Life in the Qaballah. It is sensed through the nostrils, and it is this awareness of breath which allows a person to develop control of direction of breath. It is the first basic introduction to the subtle science of breath.

By the purification, development and control of this breath all five aspects are developed.

Just as the breaths constantly adjust equilibrium under everyday circumstances, so they will develop in a human being who consciously attempts to work with breath through the first, earthly, form. By working out the directional pattern (using the five purification breaths) and by other exercises, the more subtle 'breaths', 'angels' or 'elements' can come into play in an adept's life.

There are atoms in man's body which form a certain organ, which are more or less active in different rhythms according as the breath reaches them.

It is the breath which regulates this working of the body. The subtle components are the atoms which are activated in repeated vibrational patterns, which cause their form and proper functioning. Breath reaches and regulates these atoms to create harmonious health.

The atoms which do not receive the proper breath remain undeveloped, and therefore are inactive.

Much of the time, the harmonious patterns can lose cohesion without the contact of the atoms with the specific breath which is in harmony with the form and function of that part of the body.

As the centres of the body are situated in the centre of the whole mechanism, it is natural that in the average person the breath does not reach their innermost part, as it ought to.

The subtle centres in most people remain inactive and undeveloped, as the breath never reaches the atoms of these centres. The outer undeveloped breath only reaches the 'outside' of a person, and within the centres starve and wither.

The question, 'if it is natural that it should reach them, why does it not?' may be answered that it is because man leads an artificial life.

Our present task is to return to a natural state, to eliminate all influences of the artificial life which we all live, and to become pure. Then naturally all centres function fully and life is harmonious in all circumstances. Retrieving this natural condition which is our birthright is the purpose of practices, exercises and self-discipline.

If man led a natural life it would not be necessary for him to develop by certain meditation processes the qualities that are latent in him.

In the artificial life, the total human being must train him/herself to become capable of being natural. The qualities don't come from anywhere else, but are inherent, yet dormant. Meditation and spiritual practices awaken and quicken the inner centres, allowing the adept to live life fully.

In short, there are faculties in man, which, by the artificiality of his life, are closed, and man lives an incomplete life.

Life is only complete when the five inner centres are active and functioning not only as elements or breaths but as angels.

As soon as breath touches those centres it makes them vibrate and do their work.

The five centres vibrate each according to the element or angel they are related to. Thus the total capacity begins to function.

Therefore breathing exercises given to a mureed are like the winding of a clock. Once in 24 hours the clock is wound and after that it goes on without effort.

The practice is to activate, and needn't be continued all day, but daily life becomes more and more natural as a result. The basic element breaths are the first practices in breath which are given, and it is this set of breath patterns which are described in this Gatha.

FURTHER TEACHINGS

MYSTICISM: THE COLOR OF THE ELEMENTS

All objects on earth have their peculiar element which is predominant in them, although everything is made of the comingling of the five chief elements, the difference being in their greater or lesser degrees.

It is from the intermingling of the elements that all things are made. In each thing, object or being, one of the five elements shows itself to be predominant. This can be seen by the seer quite clearly.

Not only in the substance, but also in the liquid, even in the gases we can trace this.

By observing the phenomena of the world we can observe the predominant element in all things. Not just in solids, liquids and gases of the physical world, but also in emotions, thoughts and feelings as well.

The earth element has a yellow color, which may be seen in the earth when it is dry, and this shows that the color of pure earth is yellow.

The color yellow is associated with earth, and earth associated with dryness or a tendency to remove all other elements until the earth is left in a pure state. This 'earth' is not only soil, not the ground or the planet as we usually associate it in a simplistic manner. It is not 'mother earth' (but in an extended sense of the earth element, earth is a mother) as is usually associated, because the predominance of the earth element has given rise to these associations, yet earth as referred to here is a vibrational field or pattern (as in physics) which shows itself in the world by the color yellow.

It is seen in many flowers as well as in fruits and leaves, and especially as the other elements in them lose their influence and the earth element remains.

The action of the elements can be observed by observing nature, and the tendency of earth to be left after other influences pass away is reflected also in the burial of the dead. In vegetation the colors are obvious, and autumn shows the earth element in clear display of yellow leaves.

Therefore from red or green they turn to yellow.

It is a magical display as fruits and leaves change color as they progress through their life stages. When the fire element no longer predominates, or when the water goes from them, plants show their basis in earth as yellow color.

The water element is green, which may be seen in the water of the sea and in the effect of the rainfall on trees and plants.

Water reflects, and the green color of water is, in a sense, a reflection of heaven on earth. In its nature, water is clear or white. In action, however, water is green and wherever green color is seen, there is the effect of water as the predominating element.

Yet water in its pure state is white, which may be seen in clouds, in pure streams, and in snow.

However, the presence of the color white does not always indicate the water element, only in some natural phenomena. White also indicates light, which is all colors.

The fire element is red, and not only in the rising and setting of the sun or in the burning coal is it noticed, but even in a hot substance such as pepper.

The red in sunset and sunrise shows the fiery quality most strongly, and without flames the coal still burns with fire. All things red show fire predominating in influence.

Also in the face of man, during a spell of anger, this color appears, and even the eyes become red.

Red dominates the face in anger most clearly, and the fire of emotions shows in the physiological changes of the body, with the face as a most sensitive indicator.

The air element is blue, which may be seen in the color of the sky, which is its abode.

The blue of the sky, which changes subtly and continuously, is created not by a solid dome above but by the subtle accumulation of air until it is seen as blue. This color is most delicate, least solid.

Even contact of the air with water makes the sea blue.

When there is little earth, the clear water reflects only the sky, becoming blue as in the deep oceans far from land.

The marks of this element, when predominating, are seen even on the tongue and lips of a person.

In human nature, the blueness of lips and tongue and feeling cool to the touch reflects the activity of the air element. It can be seen in the face, as can fire. Water is seen but not as a color in the complexion, only in the eye color. Similarly with earth, except in grave illness. Earth and water colors are more seen in vegetation, fire and air in human complexion and coloring.

It shows itself on the top of flames in the fire; this is when the fire turns into air.

Wherever blue is seen, there is contact with air. Some things become blue as they become air. Fire becomes air, and the place where it does this is a most explosive event.

The ether is smoky in color.

This element is different from all the others, being a combination of them all. It has no real color and is indistinct.

It is the comingling of all elements and even the origin of all.

Without the elements, ether would not exist; it creates them, joins them, yet is undefined itself.

It is as the color of mist.

Mist is like mystery.

The different grades of its activity have assumed different colors: therefore it is all colors and no color.

All the elements are sprung from ether in a subtle evolution of vibration - from ether comes air, from air comes fire, from fire comes water, from water comes earth. These are the different grades of the activity of the ether, which mysteriously controls yet remains apart from these activities. Ether is active according to the activity of the four other elements, and when they are inactive, ether is inactive also. Within ether, all live and move and have their being.

The colors of the rainbow represent the different colors of the elements collected together as one embodiment of ether.
    The synthesis of the elements produces only the indistinct colorless ether. The expression of these elements creates the colors of the rainbow.

Mysticism: The Form of the Elements

The forms of all objects tell the seer of their origin, and why a certain object is round, and why another object is square may be understood by the tendency of the element to manifest toward its peculiar direction.
    The direction of the elements shows itself in three-dimensional representation as varied shapes and relationships. The predominant element shows its strength by directing the shape and form into its own likeness. This energy pattern can be observed to tell of the element most active at the time of the object's formation.

For instance: Spreading is the quality of the earth element; therefore, the earth is always seen as something spread out, and all elements in which the earth is predominant are square.
    Here the three-dimensional holographic image of the predomination of the earth element in objects as cubes, rectangular shaped buildings (for example) can be seen as simple geometry. The square represents the earth. The spreading quality of earth could almost seem a downward tendency, but in reality it is the long flat horizontal line which represents the final result of this spreading.

Water has a tendency to flow downward, and all objects belonging to the water element lean downward.
    Weeping willows droop down, imitating the water they grow beside. The downward flow of water can be seen in various lines and forms.

No simple geometric representation of water is given here, no 3-d form, just the tendency, the idea to look for a downward falling, flowing quality.

The fire has its tendency to rise, therefore the flame goes up, even the smoke rises, and all objects in which fire predominates will show in them a rising tendency. The circular form is significant of it.

All standing, growing upward, jumping, reaching up, stretching, rising, all these show fire. Its energy directly opposes the downward flow of water, and must also overcome the spreading horizontal line of earth. Fire has extra energy for this, it is quick. All upward vertical aspiration is directly fire. The circle represents fire more like a spiral - like the spiral of the zikar.

The air has in its nature a zigzag direction, and all things concerning the air are zigzag.

One side, then the other, with rapid changes. The exact zigzag form may not be seen, but envisioned holographically, the zigzag quality of atoms and molecules of gases can be seen represented outwardly by the movement of the air.

But ether has no particular form, and all forms are originated from it. Being the finest, it is above limitations.

Form is a limitation, and from ether all forms spring. That which is beyond form can be sensed as ether.

Mysticism: The Direction of the Elements

The five elements, earth, water, fire, air, and ether are in fact grades of the abstract life in its gradual activity, and every element is distinguished by its form, direction, color and nature.

By understanding the form, direction, color and nature of things, events, persons, beings, all, the abstract life is also understood. Seeing through the physical existence gives the student of the elements an opportunity 'to know and understand life better'. These five, being modes of vibratory patterning or grades of being, can be seen as distinct entities with readable characteristics. The unseen world is the abstract life, and it can be known here in the seen world by the clues given concerning the elements. These elements or angels are conceived according to the awareness of the adept. They are the vocabulary of all life.

The direction of the earth element is level and the nature is spreading, therefore the smallest island in the sea in time grows to be a big island.

The long horizontal stretch of land, the line of beach, the flat mesa, show the spreading nature of earth. It spreads gradually and imperceptibly. Time matters little for in all things earth eventually extends itself even when other elements are gone.

The direction of water is downward. That is why rain falls, water falls from the springs and water is found below the earth.

Any gesture or tendency to bend downward shows the water element. This is a gradual motion only if there is obstruction, otherwise water rushes downward, even below the earth.

The direction of fire is upward; therefore the flame and smoke rise, and the sun, the centre of all heat, is up above.

Fire is going upward vertically, and quickly. The sun is the centre of heat high in the sky, all that has fire in it rises up, stands tall, reaches up to the heat and brightness of the sun.

The direction of air is zigzag; that is why the weather changes from time to time.

The air has no particular destination but reaches as many places as it can. It simply changes and shifts continuously from one direction to another, including in itself all the other directions but with no continuance in any way. Weather is used as a living metaphor, the earth and all life being also a living metaphor, to demonstrate the action of this abstract life.

The direction of the ether is not particularly perceived because it is still.

Ether is the clue to the inner all-pervading life.

It is the grade of activity which changes the still ether to air, and so changes its direction and nature.

From the eternal stillness of ether comes a little movement, a shift into a directed energy. From containment within comes a small wiggle, a sigh, a breath, the beginning of a word. Ether is no longer ether but has become air. Thus the activity of the air, clashing by the zigzag direction, produces electricity, the fire element of which may be seen in lightning which is zigzag in form. Observing nature shows the inner relationships of the elements in the abstract life. The wiggle becomes zigzag motion in many directions, with many such movements naturally stirring each other up, causing more activity until it crashes together and changes state, becoming no more air but fire.

It is the activity of the fire element which rises above as clouds and turns into the water element and falls as rain, as the heat of the body is the cause of perspiration and the heat of the mind accounts for tears.

The upward activity of fire accumulates above or in a sense of pressure which builds until it releases a downward direction of force. This of course is the water element. Once again, Inayat Khan uses nature as a metaphor for these workings of the abstract elements.

It is the activity of the water element, which solidifies and produces salt and minerals of different kinds, which develops into rocks and mountains and then descends and makes them a plain which is the part of earth. This shows the origin of earth in the source of water.

Water, going lower and lower, solidifies to salts and crystals, which then become more dense as rocks and eventually spread flat as earth. Actually, the vibration rate slows as water descends, creating a 'low pressure' which eventually appears to be a standstill. Then that which stands still spreads outward in the horizontal line. So the original impulse is carried through to final manifestation.

All these directions may be seen in the breath by one that can realize what element the breath is emitting at a certain time.

The adept learns to sense the direction of the breath, and in doing so, becomes able to recognize the predominating element at work. The changes in the breath are changes of element.

The breath changes its element so many times during the day and night, and, if in right order, it does not miss the right succession of the elements.

A remarkable phenomenon! In which the breath cycles through the microcosm of creation several times day and night! When totally healthy and natural, a person's breath recreates manifestation many times each day. When in harmony with the circumstances of life, these too are made more and more harmonious by the correct circulation of the elements in the breath.

From this the seer knows all about his body and mind and the body and mind of another, and, according to his development, he gets an insight into the past, present and future.

By sensing the elements in the breath all things are made clear. Insight is a natural consequence of this understanding of the direction of the elements in the breath. This knowing is all by sensing the breath and its harmonies and predominant tendencies. It is a natural feeling and not at all forced or analytical. As natural as seeing.

Mysticism: The Relation Among the Elements

The elements are related mostly to their nearest element: earth with water, water with fire, fire with air, and air with ether.

The elements seek association with their nearest element, but not with a lower vibration, rather with the higher. So water, sought by earth, seeks relationship not with earth but with fire.

Water fertilizes the earth and makes it fruitful, and heat projects water in its liquid form and keeps it from solidifying.

In the examples given here and to follow, the nature of the elements is shown in the relationships of nature. Each element receives help and sustenance from the one "higher". So water gives earth the sustenance for growth, fire helps water from becoming overcome by earth.

The tides depend upon the cosmic heat; in other words, the light of the sun reflected in the moon controls them.

In this way, water is influenced by fire, and made to move upward rather than down (its natural propensity.) Fire is seen in the heavens as all shining bodies of light which have influence on water that is bound downward without such influence.

The fire is kindled by the help of air and it is the vitality of the ether which moves through air.

In the same way, fire needs air in which to be active, for without air fire cannot burn, heat cannot be conveyed. And air, to have life, must be pervaded by ether which charges it with vital force.

Although all the elements are related to each other, yet earth and water are mated, and so are the fire and air elements, ether being exclusive.

The harmonious relationships are seen between earth and water and between fire and air. These occur naturally and are always pleasant because they are natural - with ether there is no desire or need or benefit from joining with another, for ether pervades all and controls all.

The people of the temperament in which the earth predominates will harmonize with those of the water element; people of the temperament in which fire predominates will be harmonious with those of the air element.

Each person's temperament reveals a predominant element, and this follows the tendency of that element in direction, color, form, etc. in a subtle way. It is not a 'rule' to be observed and analyzed, for there are inner indications of element influence as well, and much is unseen by those who simply study basics of element identification.

People have harmonious and inharmonious times with their friends, this is accounted for by the same reason.

As different elements predominate at different times in people, the harmony and disharmony between people can be seen in relation to these differing elements. Thus there can be harmony of elements through the breath when the temperaments seem opposed, and similarly there can be disharmony between two of harmonious temperament due to the changes in the elements of the breath.

When they have mated elements, namely earth and water, or fire and air, active in their breath, they are harmonious, and in absence of the same they lack harmony.

The harmonizing effect of a matching element in the breath can be immediately felt. Mostly this working is spontaneous, arising naturally from mutual sympathy. The most beautiful harmony comes in this way, without impediment or forethought. However, it is useful to know how to match the breath in cases where harmony is lost.

In fact, each of these elements creates out of itself its child-element and again in time absorbs it within itself.

Here begins a more subtle explanation to do with the relation of the elements. They are seen as more than interpenetrating, more than evolving by grades and degrees one from the other, but seen as wombs of one another - so the younger less developed (i.e. more limited) element springs out of the older more mature (i.e. less limited and more fluid) element. So from ether is born air, from air is born fire, from fire is born water, from water is born earth. Yet earth is absorbed again by water, water diffused by fire, fire absorbed in air, air taken in by ether. These processes are continuous.

The elements show the Creator's nature, Who creates at times and absorbs at times.
The observation of the changes of vibrational states and the creation and destruction of the elements, one into the other, gives a picture of the activity of God as the creator and destroyer.

This is explained thus in the Koran: "All come from God and all are bound to return to Him."
The ether in manifestation governs and develops the series of capacities or wombs which are the other elements. They come spontaneously from one another and return by the same route back into each other, as one cosmic outbreath and inbreath.

We see that the ether creates air, the air creates fire, the fires creates water, and the water creates earth, and yet in the water the earth is dissolved, and by the fire the water is consumed, the air puts out the flame, and ether absorbs air.
This subtle play is like Mother Kali who destroys her own children. It is the musical scales going up and down or the breath reaching out into manifestation, then absorbing all back within the unmanifest again. This repeated action is seen in the breath over and over again through the night and day.

It is this mystery which enables the Sufi to master the constructive and destructive powers of the universe with the knowledge of mysticism.
The Sufi masters the elements of creation and destruction in this understanding of the relation of the elements to one another. Providing the correct relation at the correct time. Seeing the need and filling it with the appropriate element by means of the breath. Recognizing the

ascending or descending cycle and working harmoniously with this direction, not attempting to work creatively during a destructive cycle, nor harnessing the power of the cycle during its opposition. Also, recognizing the moments when ether is predominant at the shift of the cycles, and acting accordingly.

Mastery is not only in knowing, but in knowing and doing both.
This understanding is from active working of this knowledge, from observation of and participation in nature. It does not come from study alone.

Mysticism: The Direction of the Elements

The direction that every object takes through its manifestation shows in it the nature of its predominating element.
By observing life around him/her, the adept recognizes the elements at play in all objects.

All things that bend show the water element.
Water with its downward direction causes things to bend and bow. Suppleness, curves, giving in to another, show water.

All things which spread in a straight line have earth as their predominating element.
Straightforwardness, unmovable fixed waiting and spreading, linear consciousness, time as a line stretching from past to future, show earth.

All things which rise and grow upward show in them the fire element.
Tall trees and grasses, standing on two legs, flames, volcanoes, skyscrapers, show the fire element.

All things which develop in a zigzag direction show in them air.
The flight patterns of birds, the different winds and weathers, lightning, plant leaf forms – especially the edges, show air.

And things which are hidden, and are incomprehensible or in a mist show ether predominating in them.
Fog, early morning mist, circumstances, subtlety, show ether.

It is fire, in man, which makes him rise against another.

The elements show not only in physical ways, but also in emotions. The exchange of harmonies and disharmonies occurs more quickly in emotion, and is seen in this example as fire which causes anger.

And it is water in his nature which makes him bow and bend before another.

The watery nature is conciliatory and diplomatic. Not quick to anger as is fire, the water finds its way to harmony by bowing before another, thus demonstrating the tendency of water.

It is earth in one's disposition that keeps him set and firm in his ideas, no matter how good or bad they may be.

Resistant to change like a rock, the earth nature will not shift opinion even if shown the benefit. It is strong and unbending, simply solid, often tending to dogmatic unchanging beliefs.

And it is air in the nature of man which makes his ways crooked.

Doing one thing while thinking of something else, or going one way while really going another. Air is not as easily recognized in the nature, but it can be seen and understood.

It is ether in man's nature when you cannot see what he is about.

An etheric nature does not explain itself, gives no handles or indications of its purpose of belief. It is a mystery to others.

The breath follows the same direction.

The breath goes in the direction of its predominating element. By recognizing the direction of the breath, the adept sees which element is most active.

It flows downward when the water element is predominating, and straight when the earth element is active in it; it rises when the fire element lifts it up, and it goes crossways under the influence of air; it is incomprehensible when the ether element overwhelms it.

Of all things the breath is the most responsive and reflective of the play of the elements, and shows them most of any thing or being on earth. Even the weather, atmosphere, and nature itself is not as subtle or as clear as the human breath, particularly when it is trained and observed, for then the elements broaden and expand their influence. In nature the elements are pure and freely at play, and they exemplify their characteristics in the everchanging natural world. But in human breath they are more abstract, more subtle.

And at every change of the element in the breath – which often takes place in the day and night – the mood of man changes, his desires, his inclination, his expression, even his atmosphere changes.
All the varieties of human emotion and expression can be traced to these changes of the element in the breath. This occurs continually.

And not only that, every element that he breathes has its effect upon every affair that he does, or that is done in his presence at that moment.
Not only is the individual affected by the change of breath, but also situations and circumstances, even physical health and surroundings. The influence of the elements in everyday affairs is seen in the changes of the breath and situations around these changes. From the ideal to the inner breath, to the recognizable outer breath, to the individual constitution, to the emotions and expression, to the circumstances and situations around one – all are governed by the elements. Then the return breath from all the influences of the situations and circumstances in to the emotions and the individual constitution and to the breath itself, to the inner breath and back to the ideal.
The Sufi creates total purity and ecological balance with each breath, drawing from the source to the outer manifestation and from the manifestation back to the source again, all impressions harmonized by the power of the ether in the breath.

Symbolical Activities

The earth element has been most predominant in previous symbology activities. However, it should be remembered that the balance of other elements is what keeps the earth alive. In its own element, earth is without power of attraction (although it attracts other elements, in its pure existence, the earth element does not attract the soul). Cold and dry, it cannot be formed. It is only with the vitality of other elements in combination that the planet we name "earth" is made living.

In our attraction to our planet, and our celebration and gratitude to it, we think we worship earth the element, and that is a misconception. The element and its manifestation are according to form, and the matter in-formed is actually made of many combinations of elements. The element "earth" then must not be confused by simple transposition to "soil" or "planet earth" which, although they have a predominance of the earth element, do not exemplify the element.

Similarly with all elements, the water we perceive is not the pure water element, as with fire and air also.

Understanding elemental play reveals human nature, the essence of music and art, the developments in nations and cities, the building up and denouements of all worlds. This play is the divine nature, divided in parts essential and interweaving, joining in love with all others, creating forms of sheer enjoyment, breaking out of them in glorious freedom, an impersonal ecstasy intense in purity and play.

The forms of divine ecstasy are the forms of this world, played most intensely in the human form. In love, the human being enters and becomes this divine elemental play. With one other, with many others, the elements exchange, creating new capacities for forms. It is this elemental ritual and play which creates our world, and ourselves. This mystery of life energy and divine force has occupied the sages of all time and all world-cycles. There is no higher science than the study of this nature of reality: a play of forms for divine love and life.

To work with the elements may seem to be a "lesser" or "lower" concept than to work with, say, light or some more 'lofty' approach. This misunderstanding shows a misreading of the entire process. Central to the concept of the elements in relation is a vast view of the entire world, both seen and unseen, as a great continuum, all created out of love by and of the creator for the only purpose which is again love.

The symbols can state clearly what words find so difficult to express.

The elements are not only seen and recognized in their form and manifestation in objects, nature, and human nature. They are in emotions, thoughts and aspirations. They are seen in the direction of the breath and in dreams as well. The one who is able to read the elements on earth, finds total correspondence in heaven also. There is actually no separation in the seen and unseen worlds, with the physical matter being a denser vibration of the invisible atoms of subtle thought. And the vibration of fine feeling is less dense again, until the abstract. The elements in relation all play and interplay according to their nature - whatever the density of the play. It is like a tune being played in a variety of keys - it is the same tune.

The gross matter and the fine matter in all of creation is governed by these relationships, with ether pervading all. The creative direction, as ether gives birth to air, air to fire, fire to water, water to earth, can be seen in deep meditation as a recreation of the entire manifest universe. Contemplation of these ideas gives a renewal to all creation. The return journey, as earth is absorbed in water, water in fire, fire goes to air, air becomes again ether, is also a deep meditation in which the individual aspirant becomes one with the infinite.

EARTH
- yellow color
- spreading, square shape
- direction is level, horizontal
- related to water
- mated to water
- dissolved by water
- straight line
- set and firm ideas
- straight breath
- element breath practice: in and out the nostrils

WATER
- green color (sometimes white or clear when pure)
- flowing downward
- leaning downward
- direction is down
- gradually solidifies to give birth to earth
- related to fire (opposed)
- mated with earth
- dissolves earth
- is helped by fire to remain fluid
- bowing and bending to others
- downward breath
- element breath practice: in the nostrils and out the mouth

FIRE
- red color
- rising upward
- circular form signifies it
- direction up
- fire gives birth to water
- related to air
- mated to air
- opposed to water
- absorbed in air
- rising direction

- makes one person rise against another
- breath is upward
- element breath practice: in the mouth and out the nostrils

AIR
- blue color
- zigzag direction
- gives birth to fire
- related to ether
- mated to fire
- absorbed in ether
- makes a person's ways crooked
- crosswise breath
- element breath practice: in and out the mouth

ETHER
- grey-violet, color of mist
- no particular form, no limitation
- direction not perceived - it is still
- gives birth to air
- absorbs air
- eventually absorbs all other elements
- no particular relationships, pervades all
- hidden, incomprehensible, in a mist, no direction
- you cannot see what this person is about
- breath subtle, incomprehensible.
- element breath practice: subtle, in and out the nostrils

Decoding the Symbols

The elements are vibrational patterns, basic vibrational entities or angels which are active and living throughout all of matter and life. Most elaborated in their manifestation through humanity, they are particularly evolved in the breath. The mystic learns to distinguish these subtleties of breath, in conjunction with the rhythms and emphasis described as uruj and nasool as well as jelal, jemal and kemal.

They are the manifestation of the Divine Presence and are especially visible in humanity. The human microcosm contains these powerful angels who in fact align the world. The will binds these elements into usefulness. Love is the name of this will.

Appreciation of the elements is an appreciation of the Divine Presence. No one knows the extent of this relationship which can involve the elements and human consciousness. It is the picture of lover and beloved in which the beloved is all in all.

The secret of developing an understanding of visual symbolism lies in understanding the breath. All the symbols pictorially represent the directions of the breath. Thus - the wings outstretched are the left and right breaths, the central heart is the joining of the breath.

All symbols are subtle confluences of the breath, whose image is seen in all things and in all of nature and in humanity and the stars and planets. This "breath" is not only the air we take in and out by way of the nostrils, but is the prana or life force or chi emanating in varied forms.

Symbols may be uncoded by breath in this way: Observe the symbol, recreate the symbol by means of the breath in the mind; let each outbreath "draw" another aspect of the symbol, or make the symbol golden, a symbol of light.

What if colors are used? The colors are symbolical of the different elements emphasized in the breath, and the colors, direction, form and shape all present the uncoding of the symbol.

Analysis is rich and meanings are multiple, for the feeling in breath is also an aspect. And the layers of cultural associations, mental imagery from centuries past, recent connotations, all give nuance and meaning to the symbol under study. But the simplest version of the symbolical understanding of all that is manifest comes through the understanding of the direction, color, form and intention of the breath.

Seen outwardly, it is the manifest world. Seen inwardly, it is the world unmanifest, in which all symbols are apparent and clear. But WHAT DO THEY MEAN? is the question we always ask. Their meaning deepens the more they are examined, and their importance to the wholeness of human life is that they are the image of the breath of God, in infinite variation. They manifest all the range of human emotion and aspiration. They are as present as the earth and the sky, always have been and always will be.

When a symbol has been for some time in use, its gold is no longer recognized, it is taken for granted and it is then withdrawn from the outer world and, as an in breath, is seen in the inner world.

The whole world could be seen as the inbreath and outbreath of God, in which the outbreath is the creation, the manifestation. Then the inbreath, the destruction, the return to the source. The manifest world is a symbol; the unmanifest world is a symbol. The inner world holds perfection, the outer - limitation. The ideal is created in the inner and made manifest in the outer. Subtle variations constantly occur as the ideal is created continuously.

The inner and outer worlds hold all the wealth and riches for students of symbology to explore. The study of symbols also includes those described in poetry, those manifest as musical forms, those so subtle they are veiled a thousand times by allusion, hiding in elaborate metaphor, hiding in dramatic exposition.

All telling the same tale: the description of the Beloved. God is Love, Lover and Beloved. The exploration of symbology is the love of the lover for the beloved, thus recreating again and again the divine ideal.

Observations

The complete natural human being is a balanced ecology of the elements. The rise, fall and mingling of the varied element-vibrations cause different thoughts, feelings and weathers.

The breath of those who perform the Sacred Element Ritual becomes naturally harmonious. It is in this harmony of the breath, the lights of the breath, that the power of this activity is seen. The working out of this unseen power impulses humanity to create new forms

Those who can live and observe in both the inner and outer worlds create the ideal on earth.

The entities called elements manifest all reality both physical and metaphysical, and are carriers of human impulses into manifestation. They are either controlled or controller.

Those participating see only a small part of the ceremony, most of which is being enacted vibrationally in a simultaneous harmony in the unseen world. It is from this mutual interpenetration that the regeneration of the world is assisted through Symbolical Activity.

Central to the Symbolical Activity is the notion of no separation, no separate identity, no isolated person or event or element.

ABOUT THE AUTHOR

Carol Sill (Sufia) is a writer and publisher who has been actively involved in the sufis since 1974. A grandmother of two, she currently lives in Vancouver, BC, with her husband, the artist James K-M. Her initiator, Shamcher Beorse, was a pupil of Pir-o-Murshid Inayat Khan who connected her to many of the streams of sufism including the work of the brothers Pir Vilayat Inayat Khan and Hidayat Inayat Khan, as well as the Ruhaniat originally established by Murshid SAM Lewis. Through Shamcher and his unified inspiration, from 1974-1995 she founded and co-founded several Sufi centres, retreats and gatherings in Canada, including Lake O'Hara Camp in the Rocky Mountains. She continues her element study to this day, and currently manages the Shamcher Archive, comprised of writings on sufism, energy and economics, with particular emphasis on OTEC (Ocean Thermal Energy Conversion) which provides benign solar power from the sea. www.shamcher.wordpress.com.

www.ingramcontent.com/pod-product-compliance
Lightning Source LLC
Chambersburg PA
CBHW022110160426
43198CB00008B/418